# THE ARK BOOK
# OF RIDDLES

the Ark Book of Riddles

© 1980 David C. Cook Publishing Co.

Published by David C. Cook Publishing Co., Elgin, Il 60120

90 89 88 87      10

Printed in the United States of America
ISBN 0-89191-250-9
LC 79-57214

# The Ark Book of Riddles

By Myra Shofner

illustrated by Dwight Walles

**What animal in the ark was in debt?**

*The duck. He had a bill.*

**God made a bow that no man can tie. What is it?**

*The rainbow.*

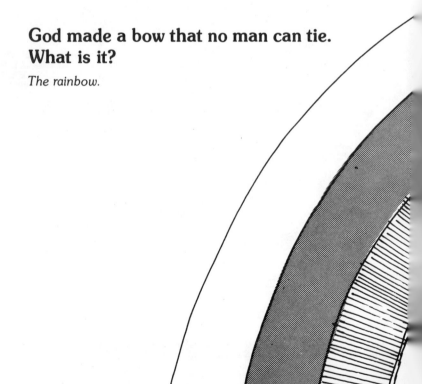

## Who brought luggage into the ark?

*The elephant. He had a trunk.*

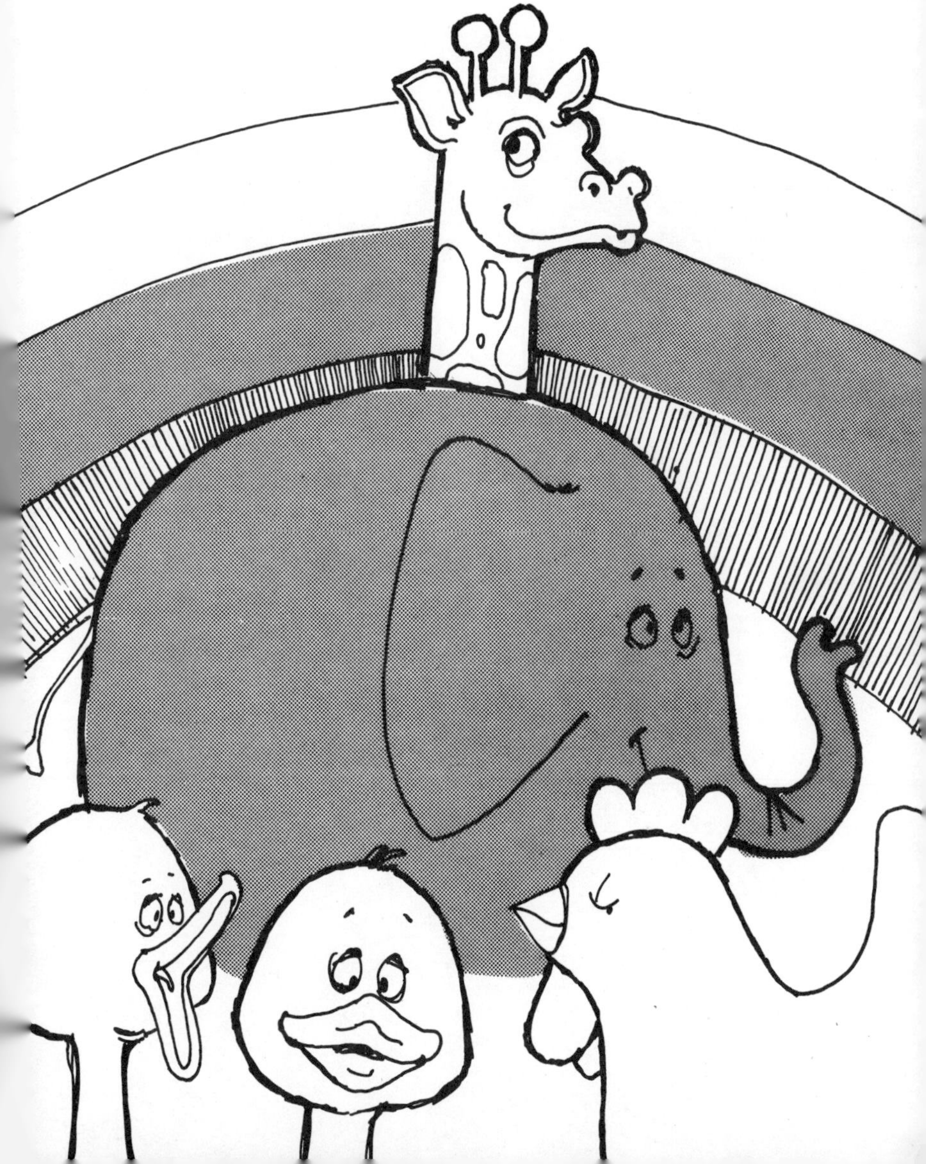

# Why is "Moses built the ark" like a left foot?

*Because it isn't right.*

**Which book of the Bible contains a part of a speech?**

*Pro-(verbs).*

**What money did Noah carry into the ark?**

*Doe and bucks.*

**Why were the horses on Noah's ark never asked their opinion?**

*Because they always said neigh.*

## What part of his body did Noah need to build the ark?

*His nails.*

## What did Noah can while in the ark?

*He preserved pairs.*

# Which son of Noah's dressed like a clown?

*His second. He was a Ham.*

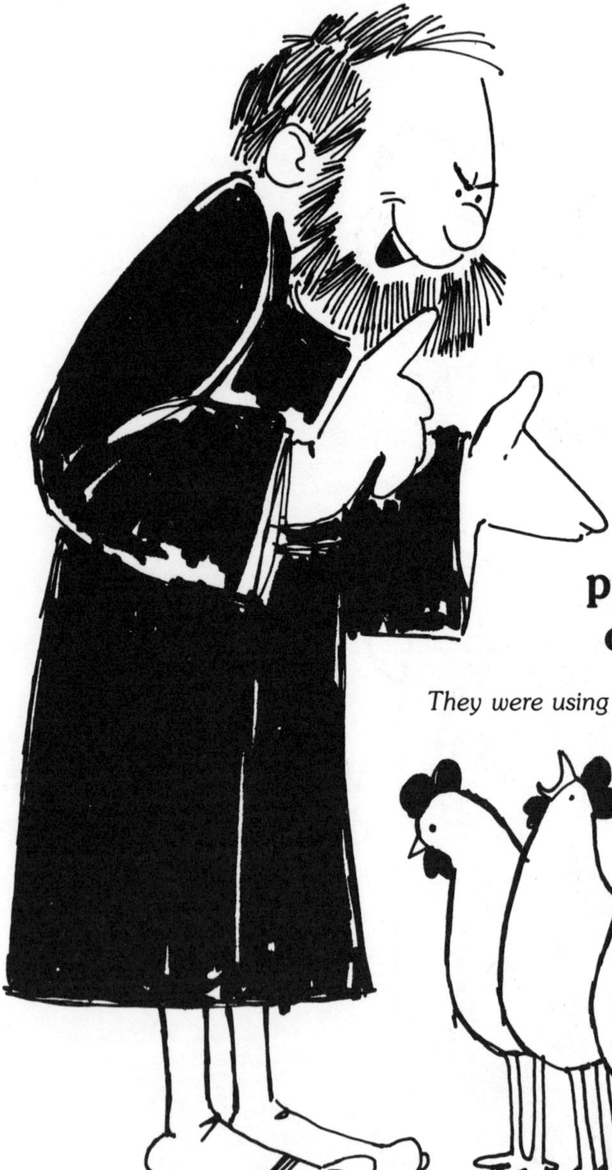

**Why did Noah punish the chickens?**

*They were using "fowl" language.*

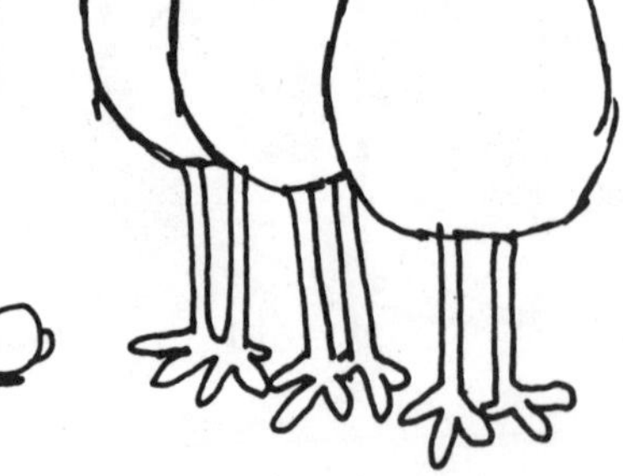

## In which state would Noah feel most at home?

*ARK-ansas.*

## Which burns longer—the candle set on a hill or the candle hidden under a bushel?

*Neither. They both burn shorter.*

## Why did Noah find the giraffes cheap to feed?

*They could make a little food go a long way.*

# What was the smartest animal on the ark?

*The snake. Nobody could pull its leg.*

## What keys did Noah take on the ark?

*Mon-keys, don-keys, and tur-keys.*

**What had an elephant's trunk, a giraffe's head, a bird's beak, and a lion's mane?**

*Noah's ark.*

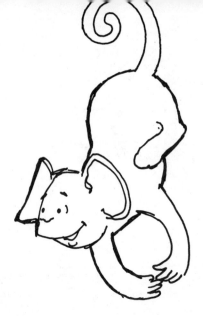

**Why did Noah have to make his own arrows?**

*Because God only provided a bow.*

**Where did Noah strike the first nail on the ark?**

*On the head.*

## Why did Noah put oil on one of his monkeys?

*He wanted to see a monkey shine.*

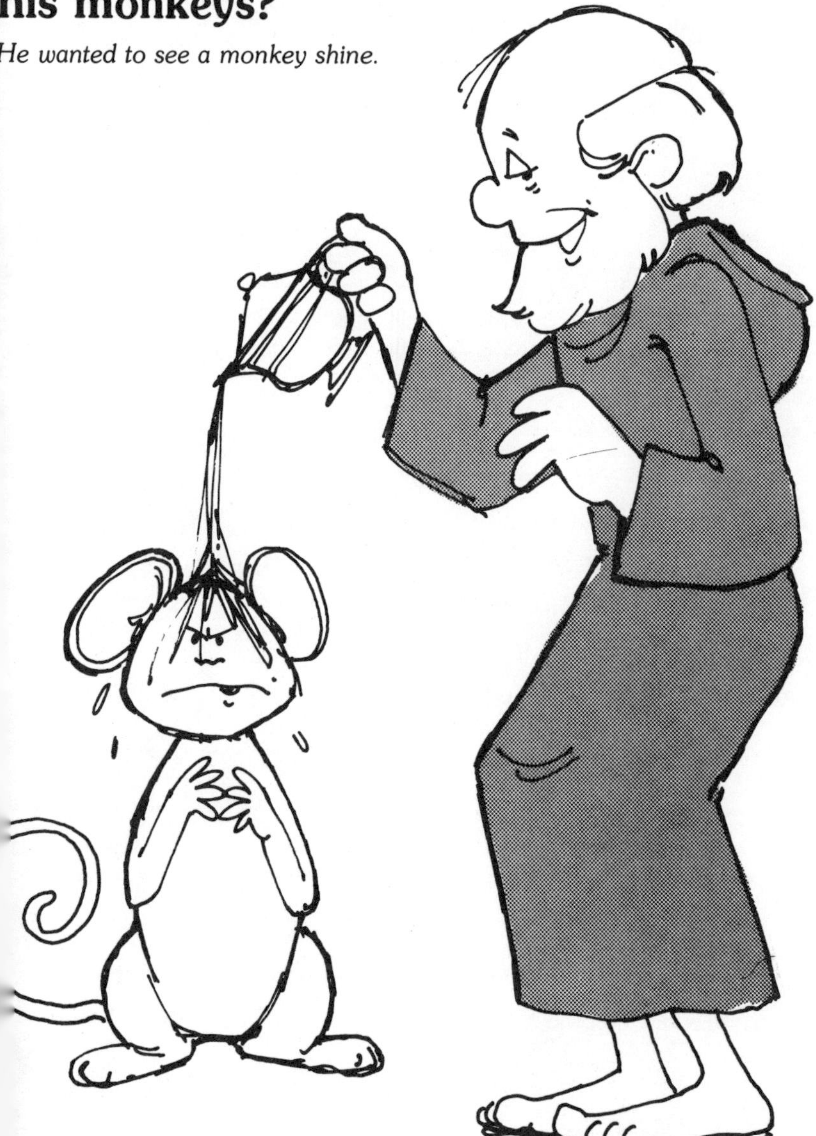

## What bird is always seen in Joshua and Judges?

*A jay (j).*

## In what sporting event did Adam excel?

*Running. He was first in the human race.*

## On which side did the leopard in the ark have the most spots?

*On the outside.*

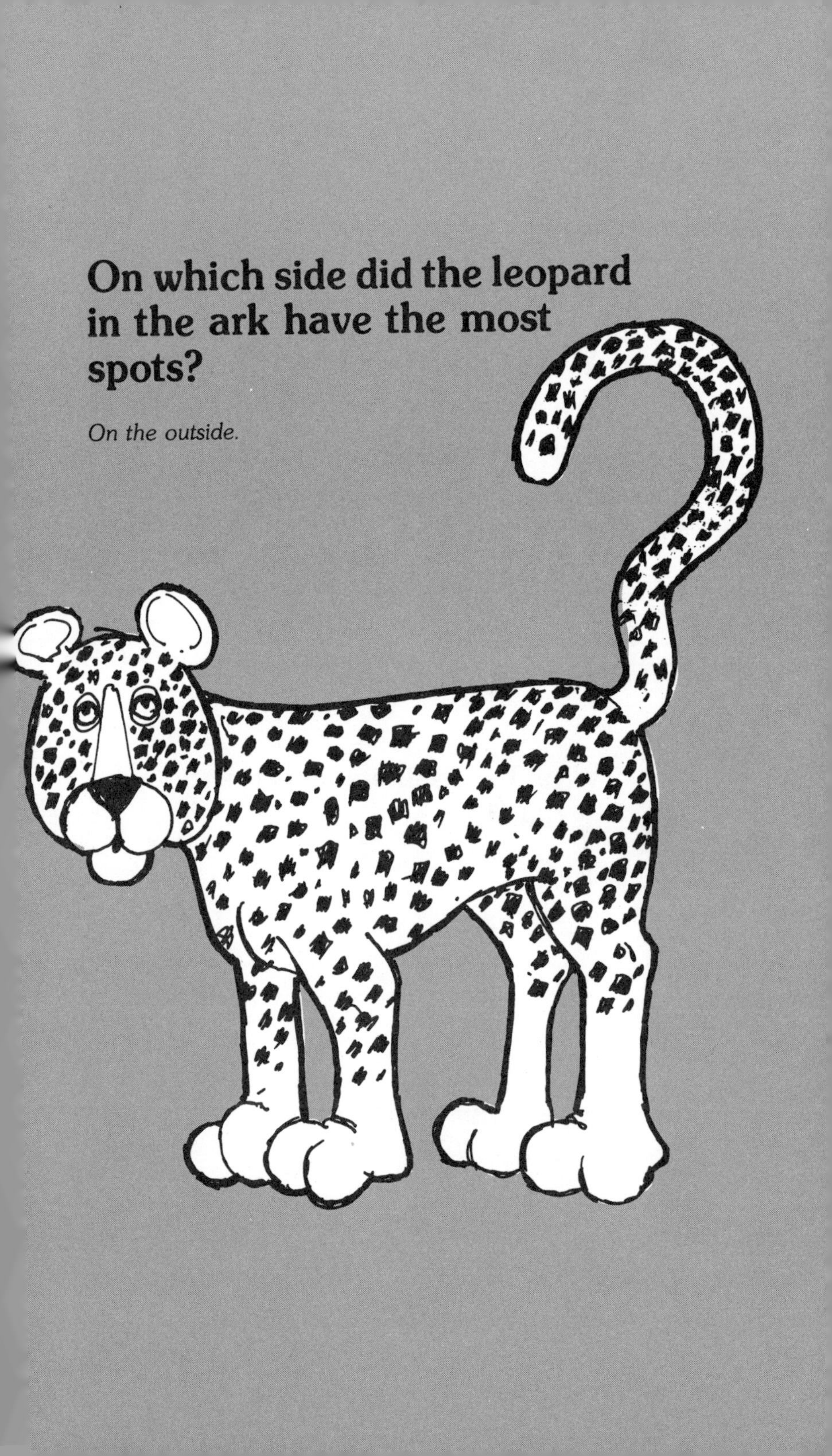

# What did God tell Noah when he asked if he could build the ark of brick?

*"Gopher (go for) wood."*

# What baseball player is mentioned in the Bible?

*The pitcher Rebekah came to the well with.*

# How many big men were born into the family of Abraham?

*None. They were all born babies.*

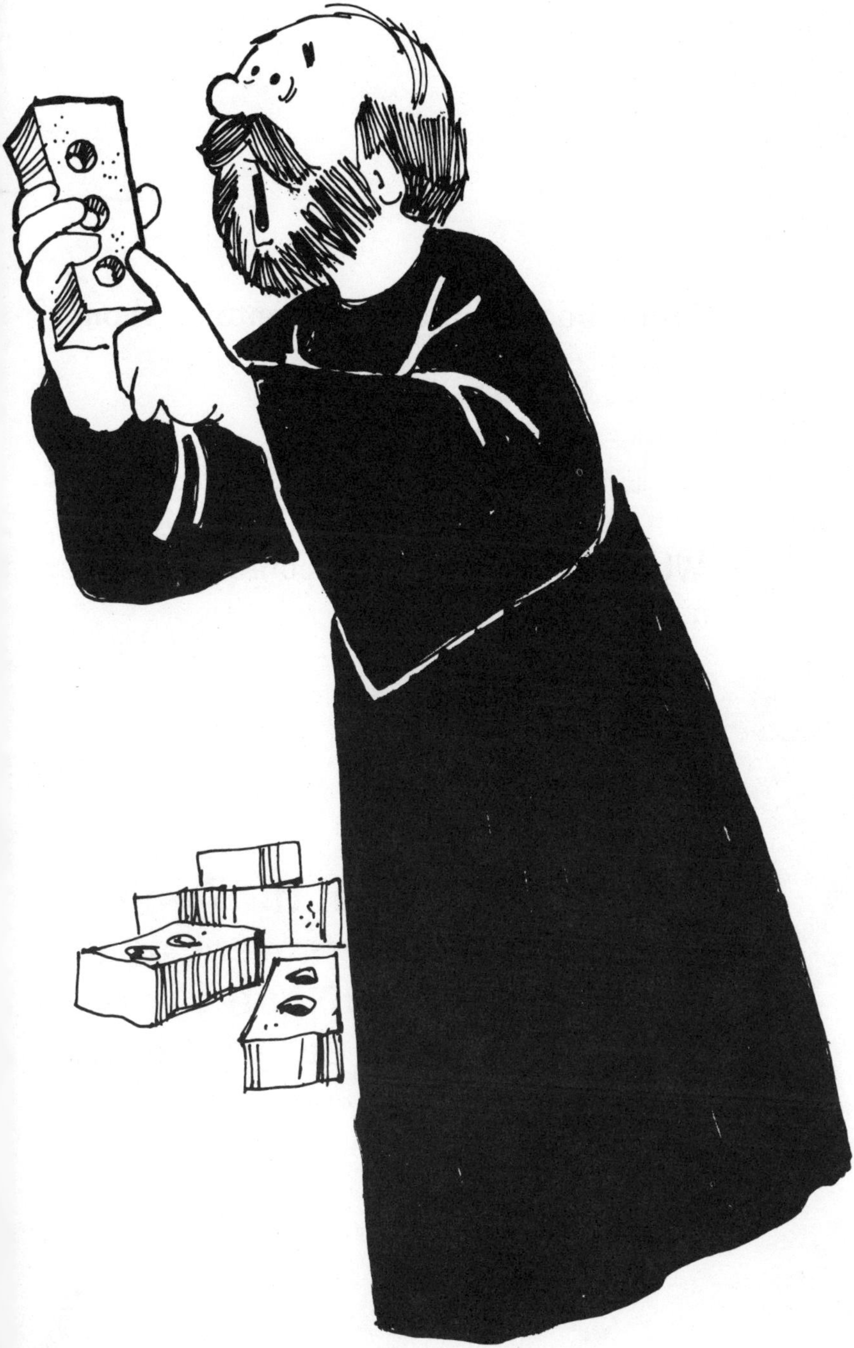

**Which book of the Bible contains money?**

*Ps (alms).*

**Which book of the Bible contains a sad song**

*(Lament) ations.*

**When the flood waters went down, was Noah the first one out of the ark?**

*No, he came fourth (forth).*

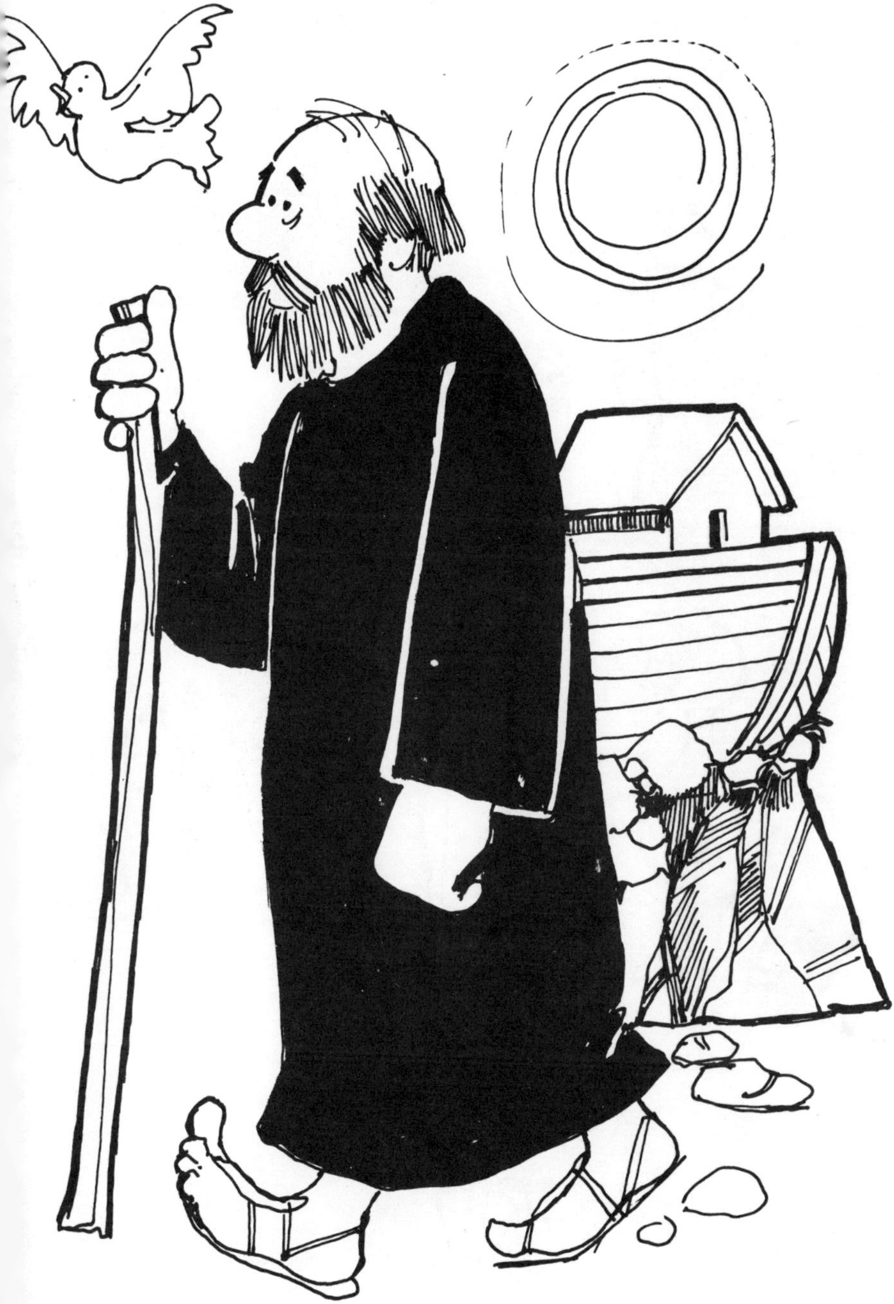

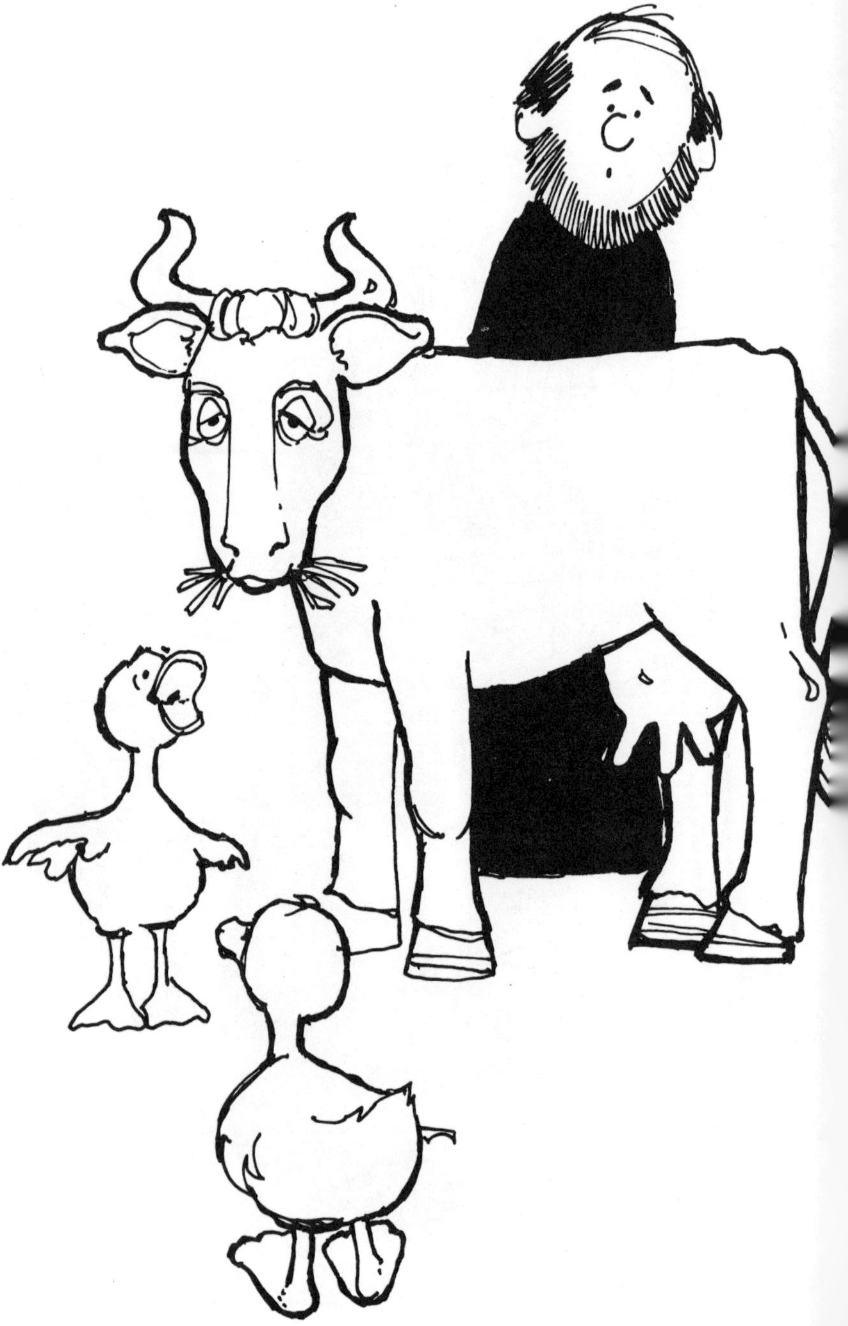

**Which book of the Bible is wet?**

*Hosea because it contains a sea.*

**If Noah got milk from the cows, what did he get from the ducks?**

*Quackers.*

**Which book of the Bible can count?**

*Numbers.*

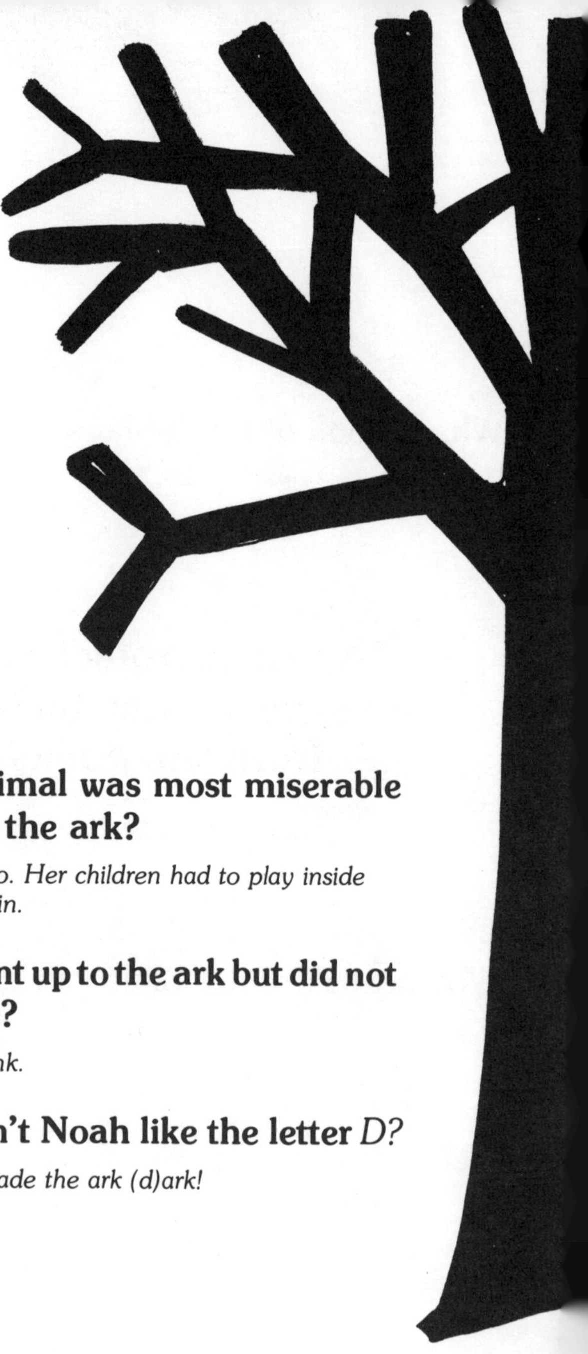

## What animal was most miserable while on the ark?

*The kangaroo. Her children had to play inside during the rain.*

## What went up to the ark but did not go inside?

*The gangplank.*

## Why didn't Noah like the letter *D*?

*Because it made the ark (d)ark!*

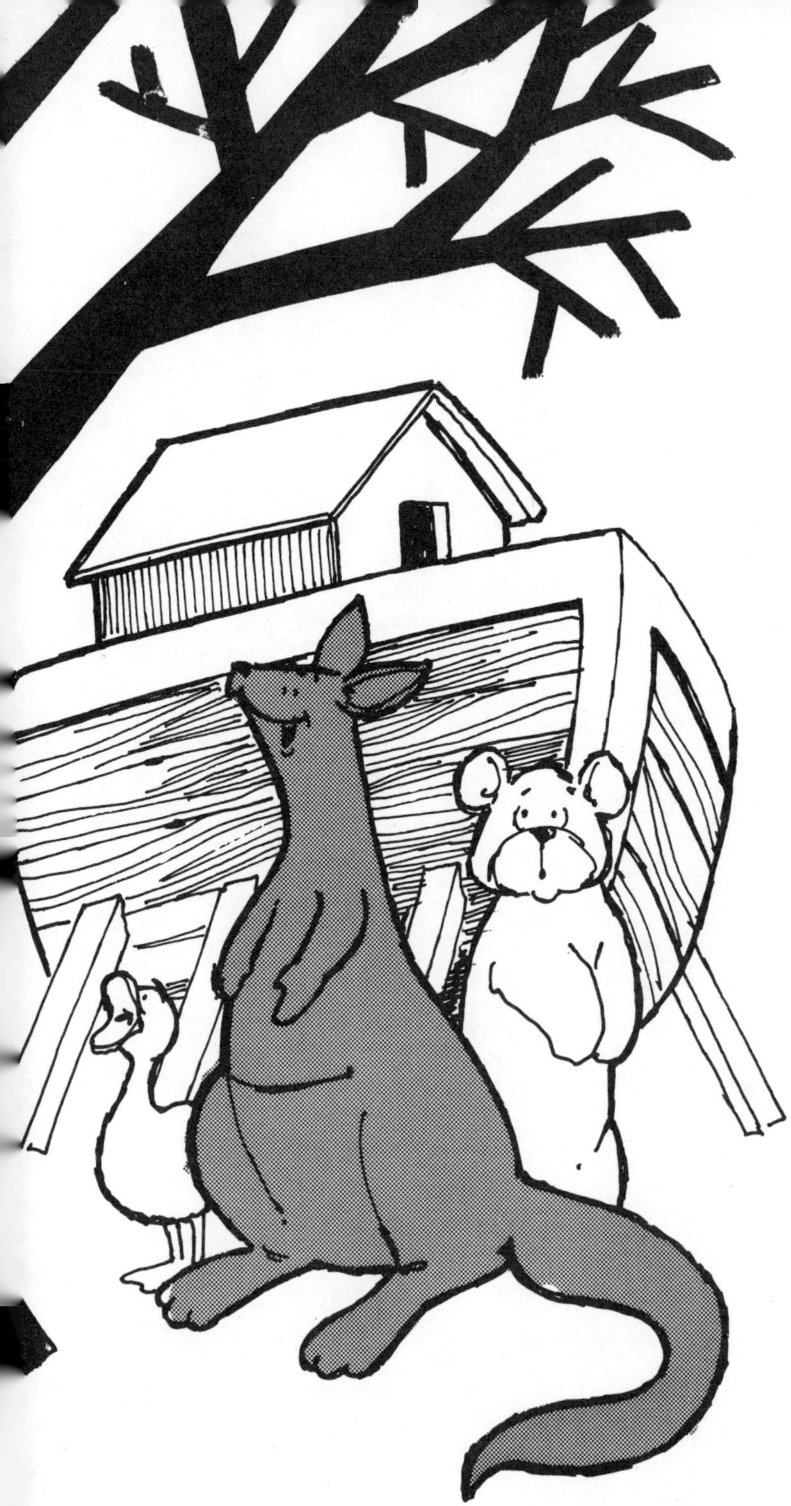

**Where does Exodus come before Genesis?**

*In the dictionary.*

**What fruit in the Garden of Eden was never lonely?**

*Bananas and grapes. Because they hung around in bunches.*

## At what time of day was Adam created?

*A little before Eve.*

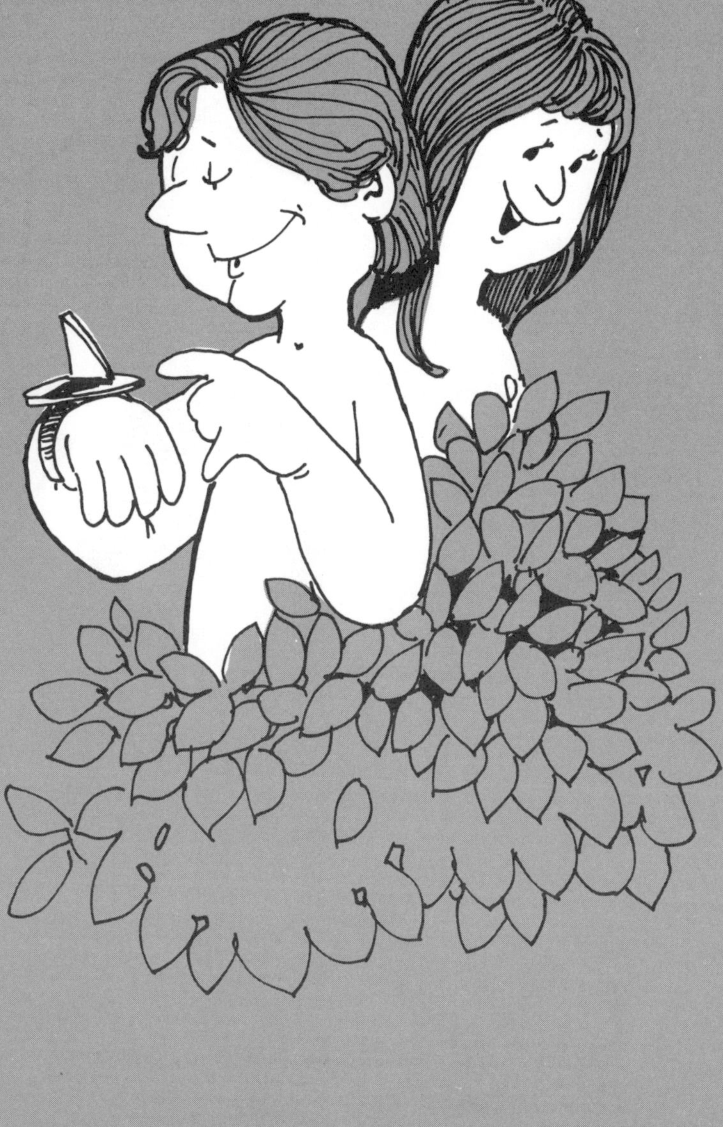

# Why couldn't Jonah trust the ocean?

*He knew there was something fishy about it.*

## How did Jonah feel when the whale swallowed him?

*Down-in-the-mouth.*

## How did Jonah feel when the whale spat him out?

*All washed up.*

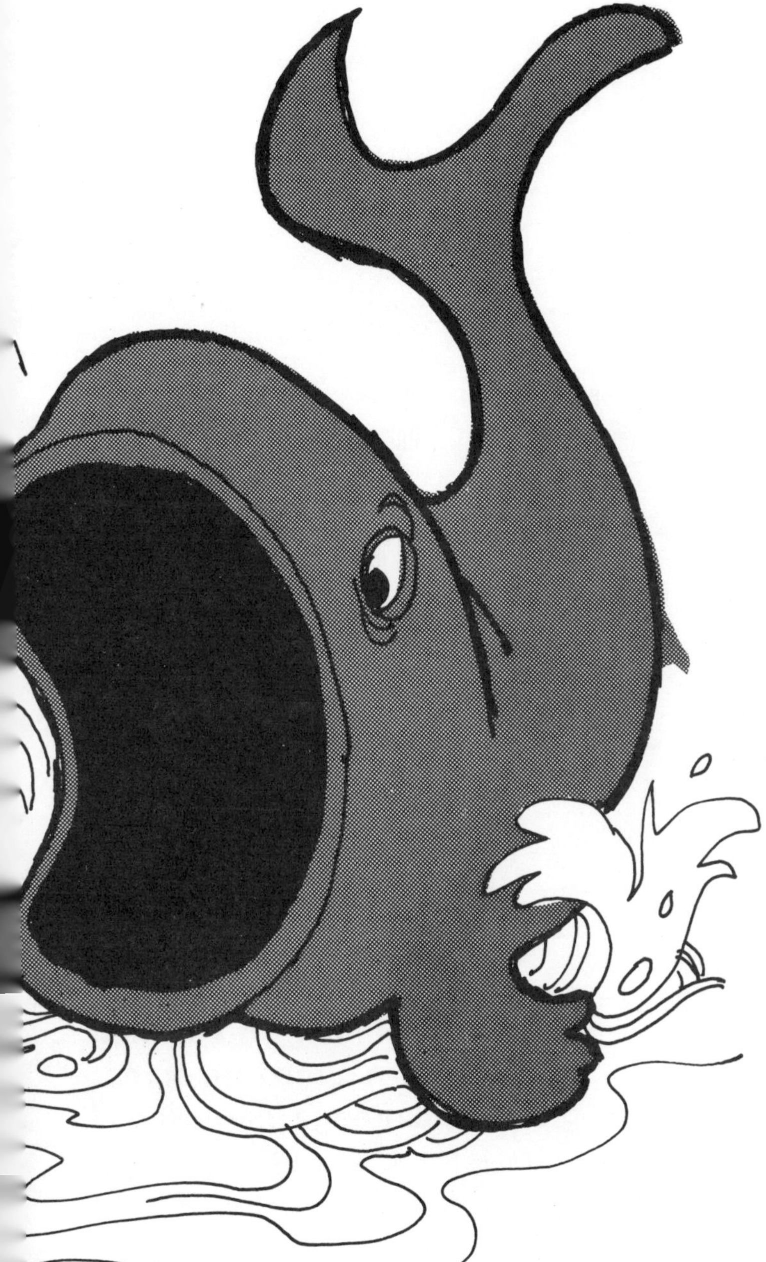

**When was the Jordan River angry?**

*When someone crossed it.*

**How is the painter who painted the barn with a mixture of red, green, and orange like Joseph?**

*They both became known for their coat of many colors.*

# What did Daniel's enemies hope the lions would do?

*Cause an uproar.*

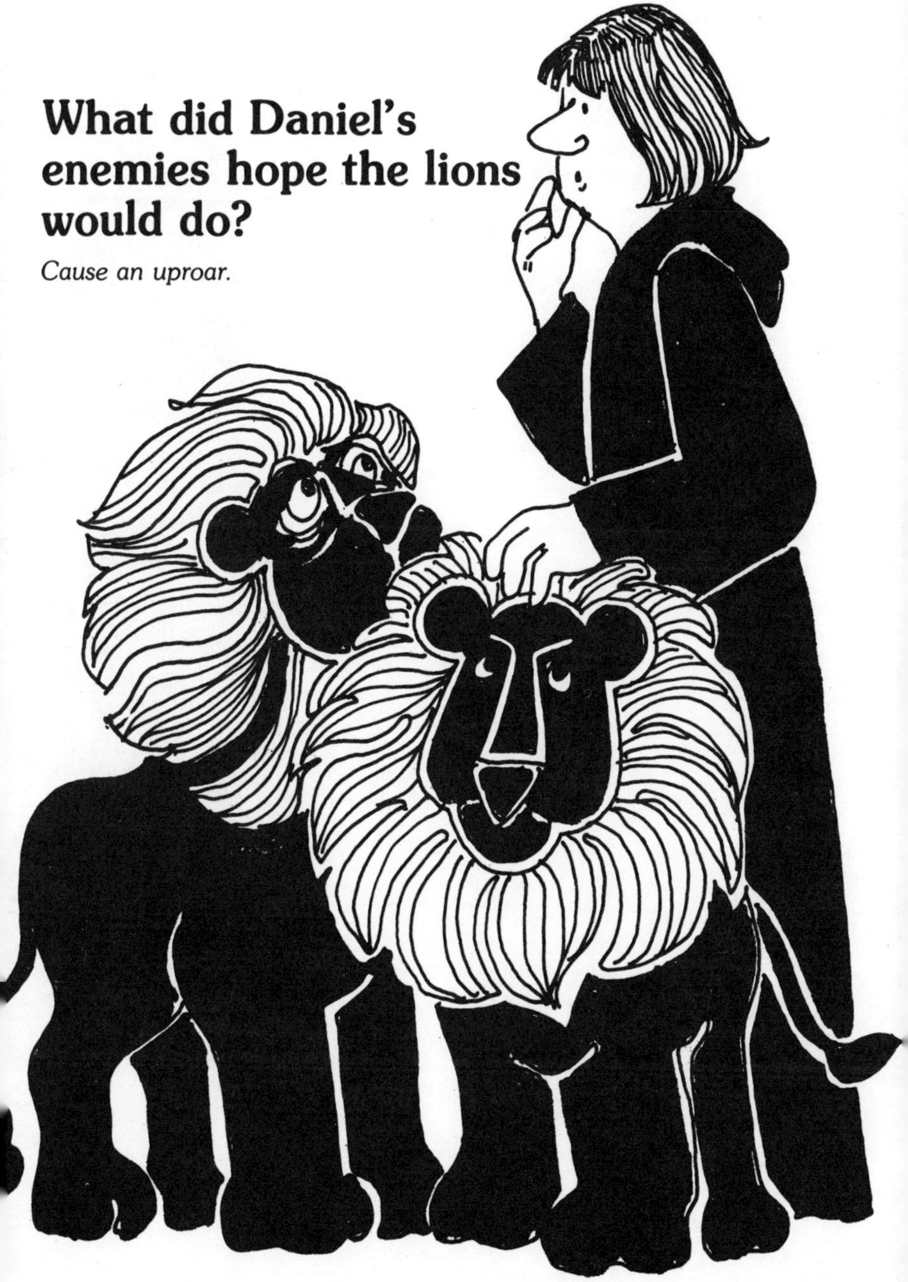

# How was Abraham like a baseball player?

*He tried to make a sacrifice.*

## Which book in the Bible travels?

*(Rom)-ans.*

**What is it that can be found in Matthew and Mark, but not in Luke and John?**

*The letter* **a.**

**On which person in the Bible was the first surgery performed?**

*On Adam when God removed a rib.*

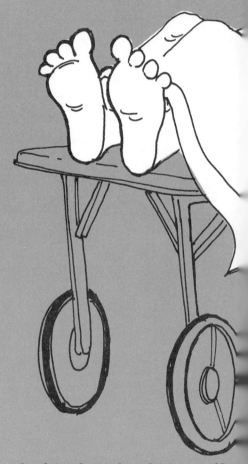

**What is black and white but should be red?**

*The Bible.*

# What does a doctor need that Job had?

*Patience (patients).*

**If Pharaoh had thrown a black stone into the Red Sea, what would have happened to it?**

*It would have gotten wet.*

# How did Job make extra money?

*He rent his clothes.*

**Why was Abraham so smart?**

*Because he knew a Lot.*

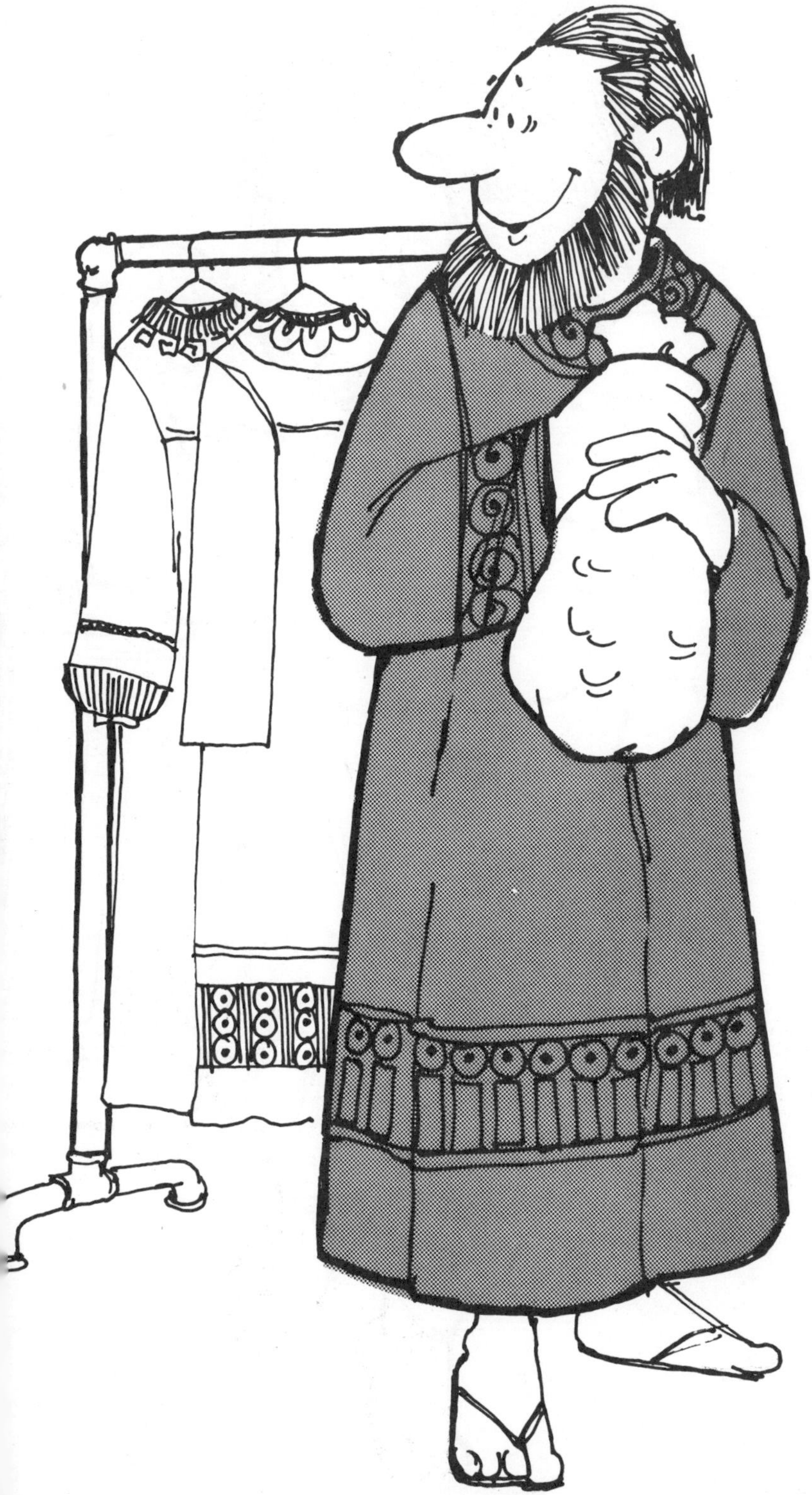

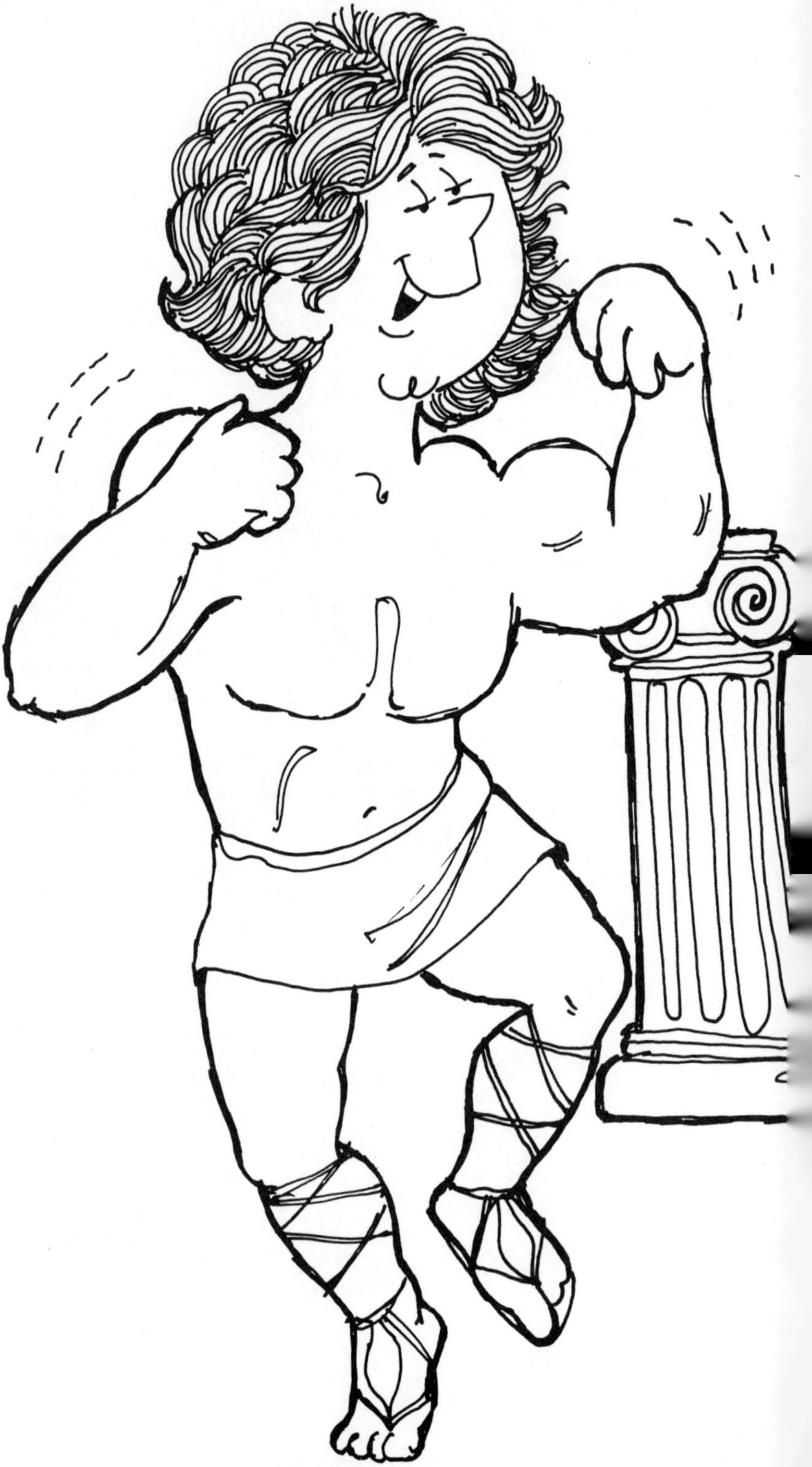

## How do we know Samson was a great actor?

*He brought the house down.*

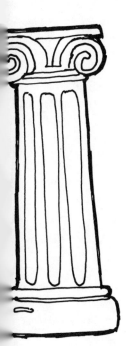

## Why did the earth weigh less at the end of the first day?

*It was lighter.*

## When was God a mathematician?

*When he divided the waters, multiplied Abraham's seed, and added to the church.*

## Which man was only twelve inches?

*Nicodemus. Because he was a ruler.*

## Which book of the Bible has a musical sound?

*Na-(hum).*

## Which book of the Bible contains something that is not good?

*O-(bad)-iah.*

## Why was it more expensive for Moses on Mt. Sinai than it was by the Red Sea?

*Everything is higher in the mountains.*

## Which book of the Bible contains an insect?

*Ti-(moth)-y.*

## Which book of the Bible contains a fruit?

*Phi-(lemon).*

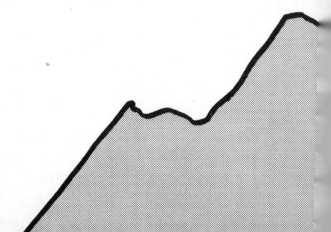

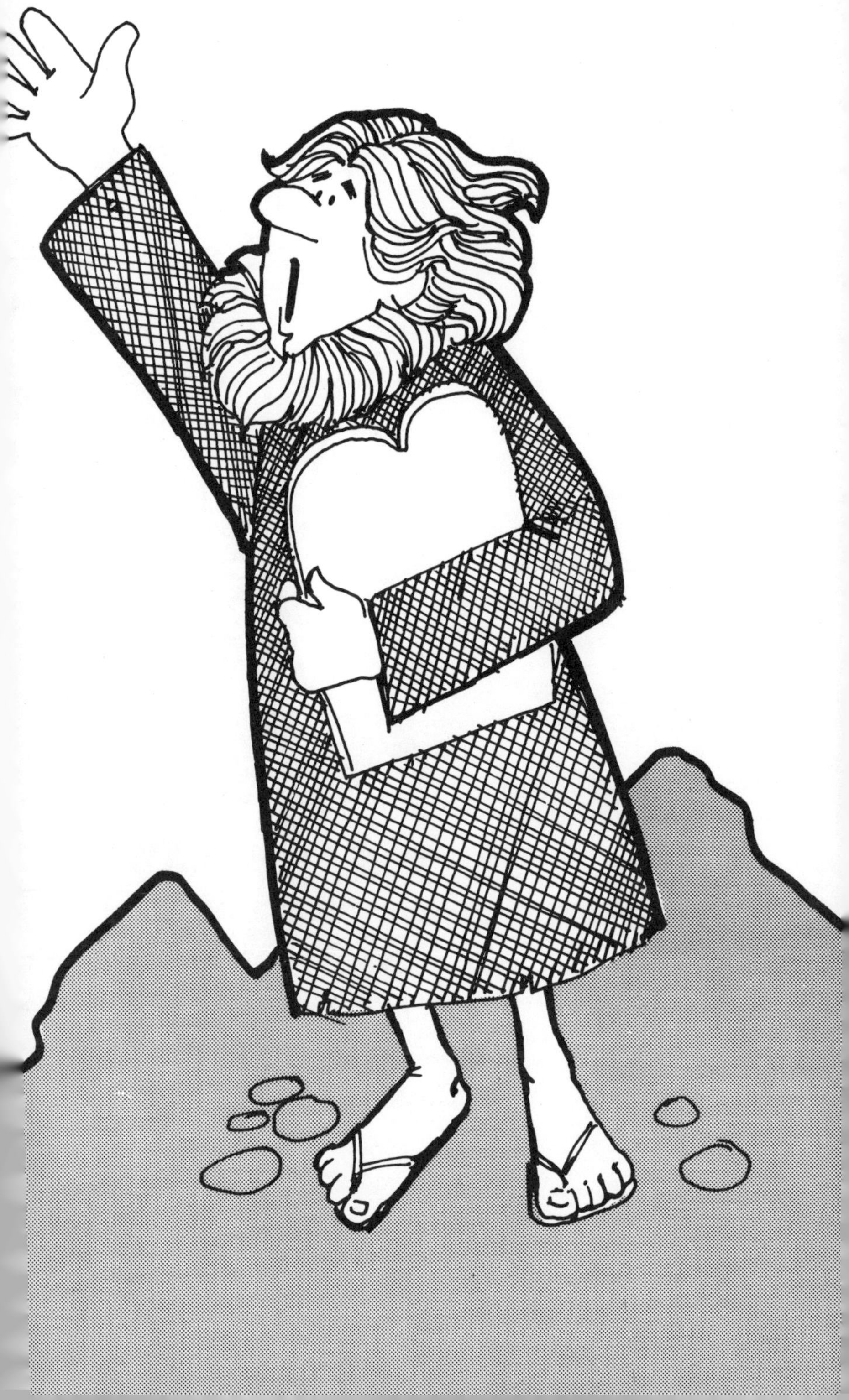

## How do we know there were newspaper reporters in New Testament times?

*Because Zacchaeus couldn't see Jesus for the press.*

# What did the boy's report card have in common with Moses?

*A Red Sea* **(C)**.

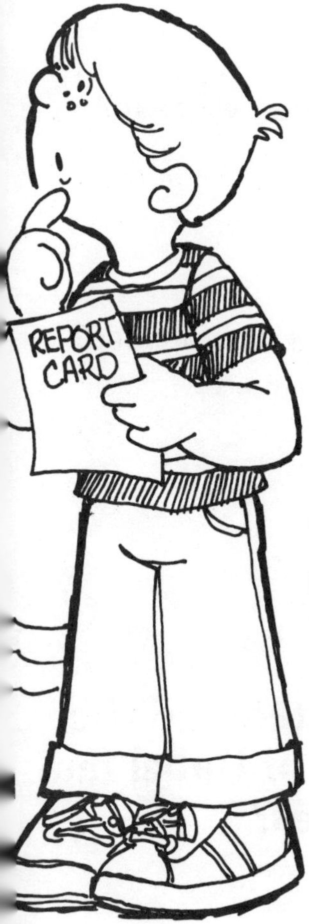
REPORT
CARD

## When is a well read Bible like the fall of the year?

*When its leaves turn.*

**Why will we get wet when we reap?**

*Because we'll reap in dew (due) season.*

**What multiplied when it was divided?**

*The lad's lunch of five loaves and two fishes.*

## In what state did the residents of Babel find themselves?

*The state of confusion.*

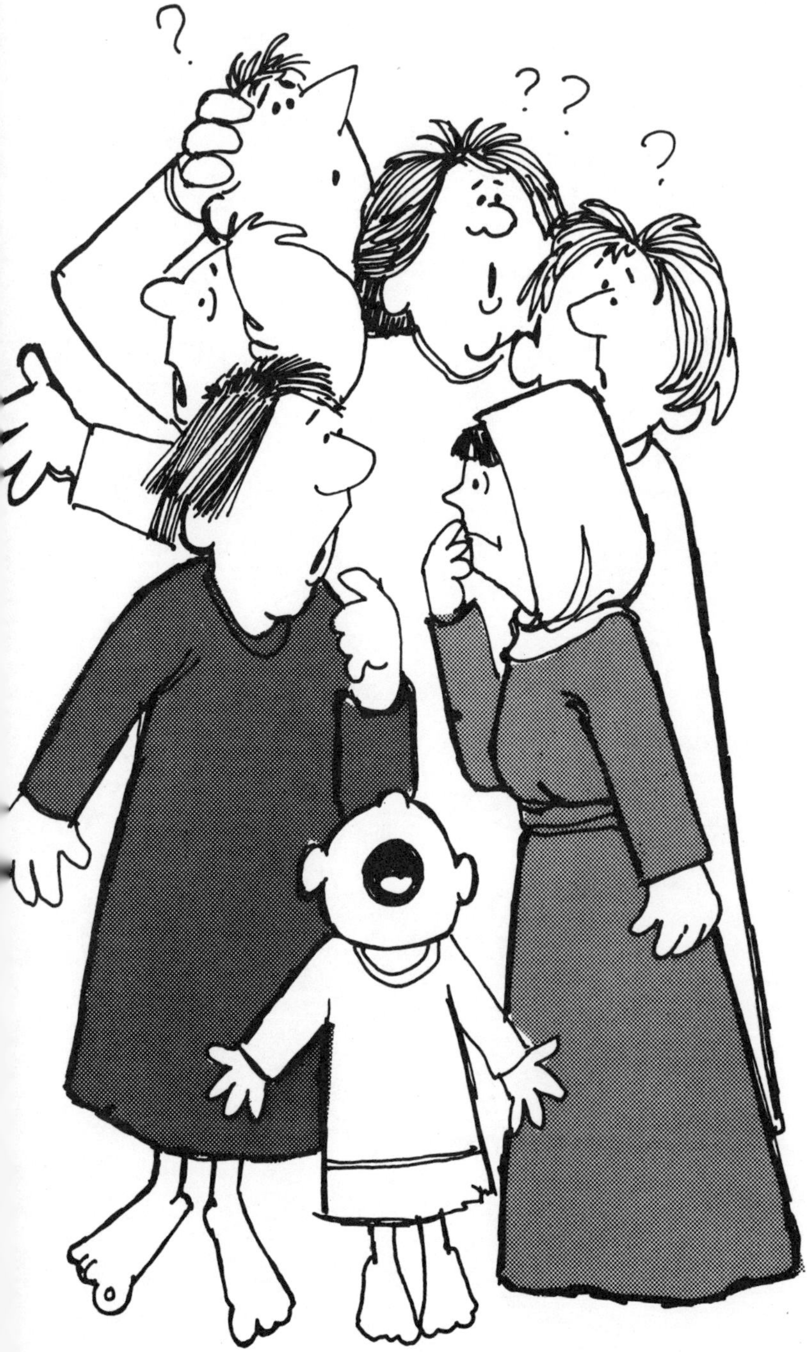

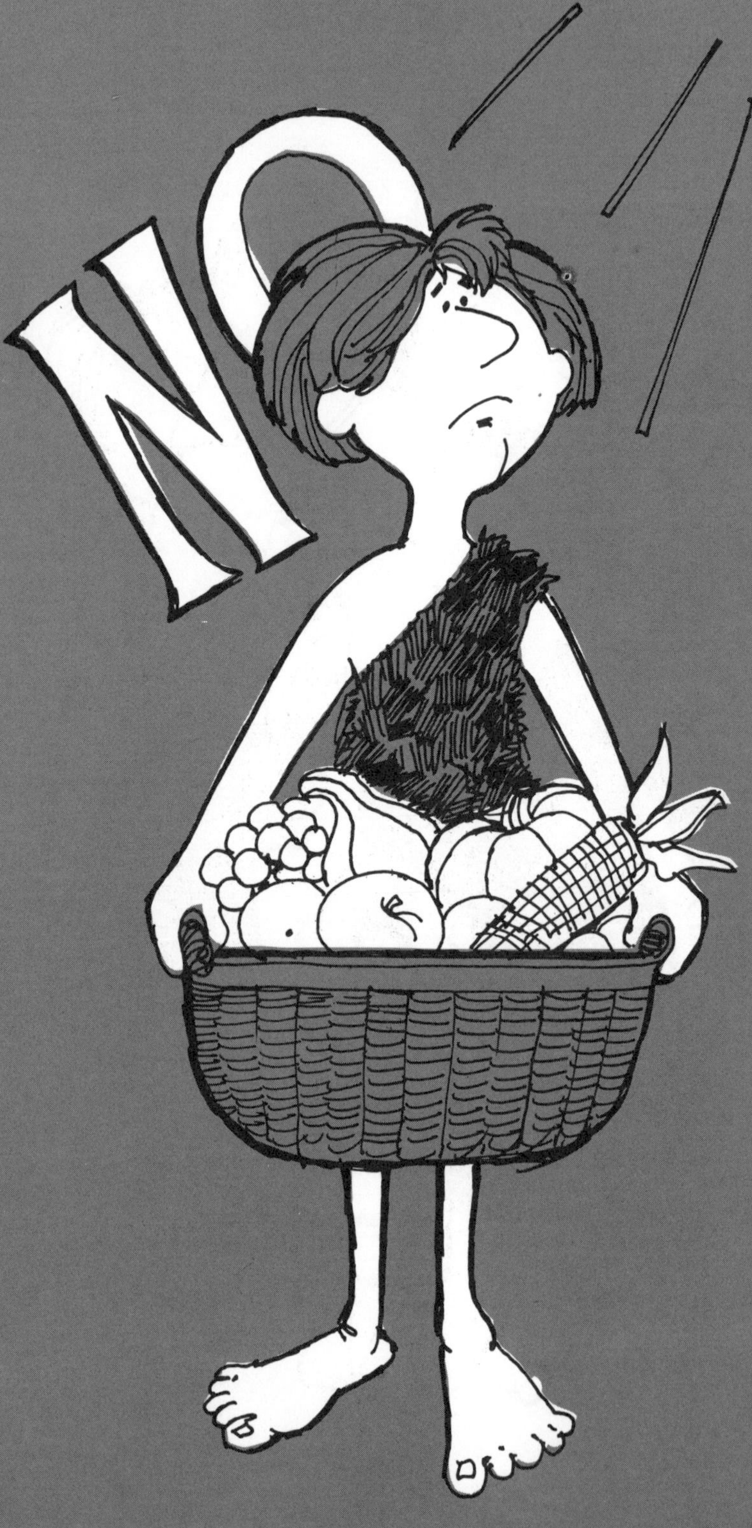
NO

**Which book of the Bible contains the opposite of profit?**

*Co-(loss)-ians.*

**Why didn't Cain please the Lord?**

*He simply wasn't Abel.*

**Which book of the Bible contains a place for fixing hair?**

*Thes-(salon)-ians.*

## Which book of the Bible contains an ugly old woman?

*(Hag)-gai.*

## Who was the man who had no father?

*Joshua. He was the son of Nun.*

## Which book of the Bible contains a part of the body?

*Phi-(lip)-pians.*

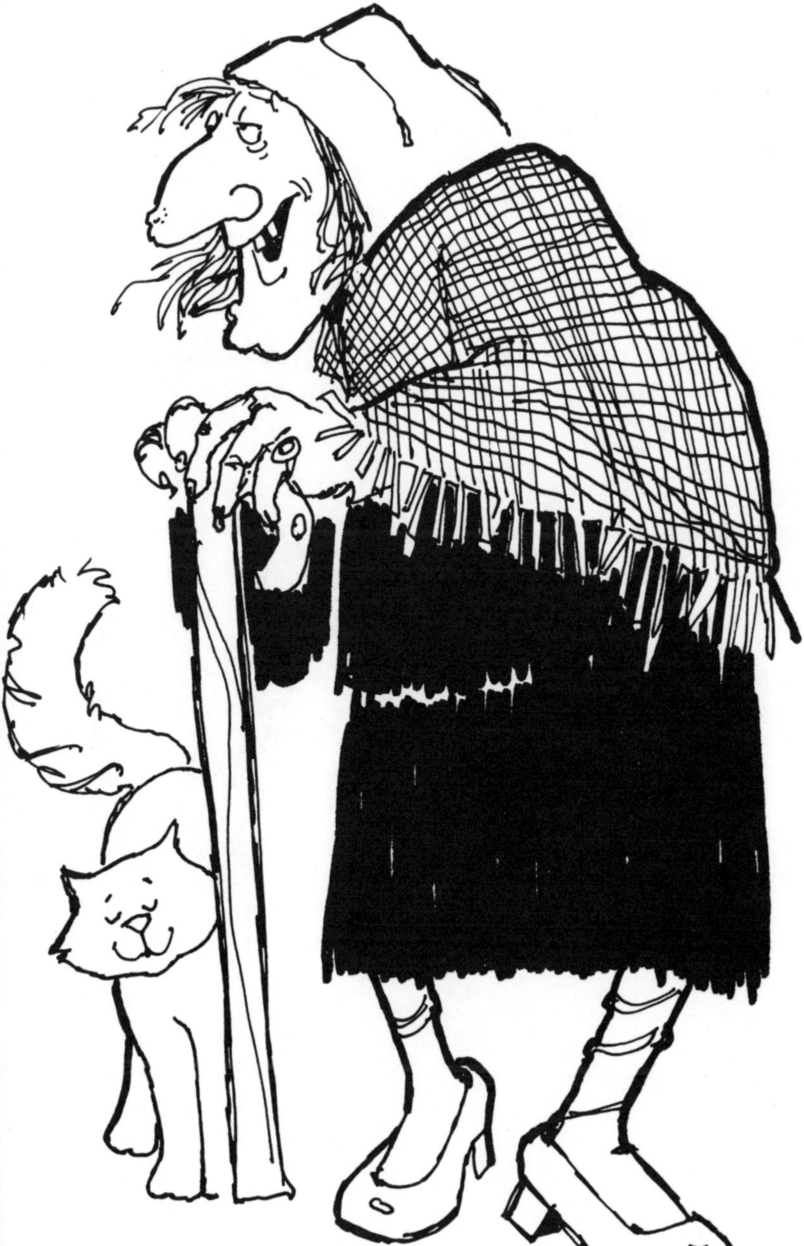

**What can always be found between the Old Testament and the New Testament?**

*The word* **and.**

# What pet of Gabriel's makes sweet music?

*His trum-pet.*

# What is old as Mt. Sinai and Mt. Moriah?

*The valleys between them.*

**What do you find only once in an ordinary book, but twice in every Bible?**

*The letter* **b.**

# How do we know Adam was a farmer?

*Because he raised Cain.*

**What book in the Bible has something every play has?**

*Acts.*

## Why did the Pharisees wear hats?

*To cover their heads.*

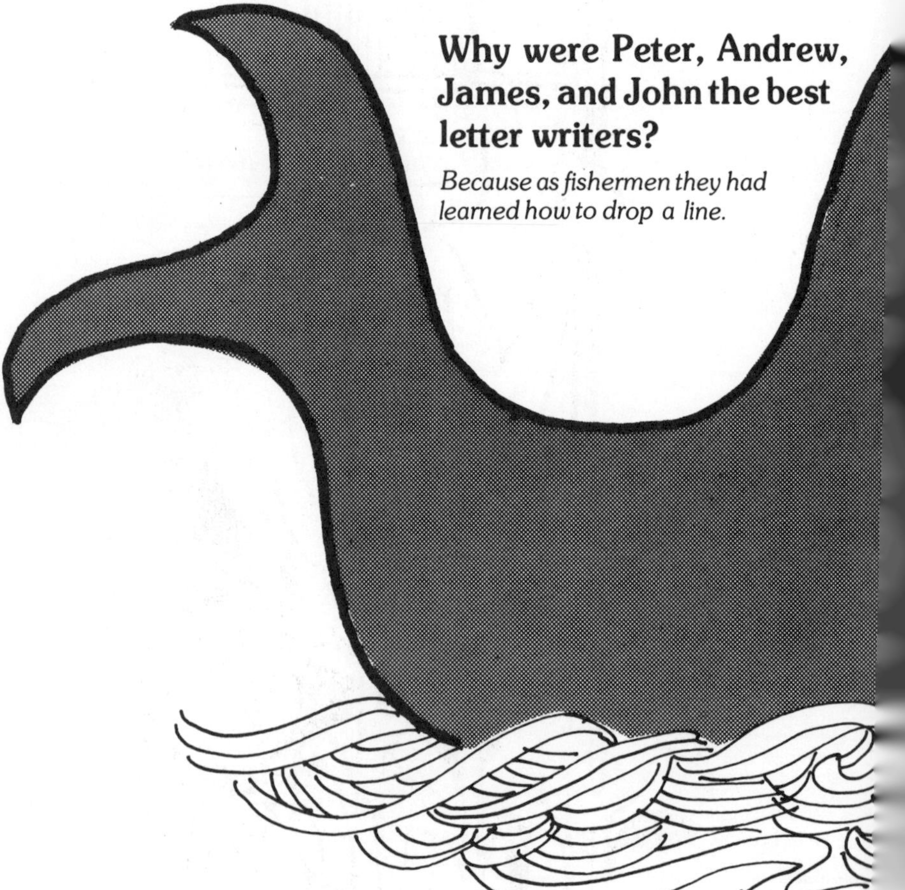

## Why were Peter, Andrew, James, and John the best letter writers?

*Because as fishermen they had learned how to drop a line.*

# What did Jesus and the whale have in common?

*Jesus had dinner with a sinner and the whale had a sinner for dinner.*

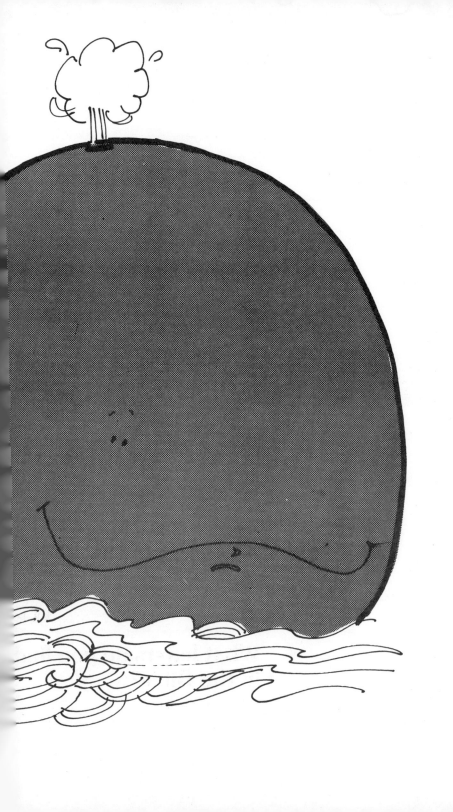

**How can you make the Book of Ruth truth**

*Add a* **T.**

**What has two eyes but cannot see?**

*The Book of Isaiah.*

**What letters do you find in the Bible?**

*T, H, E, B, I* **and** *L.*

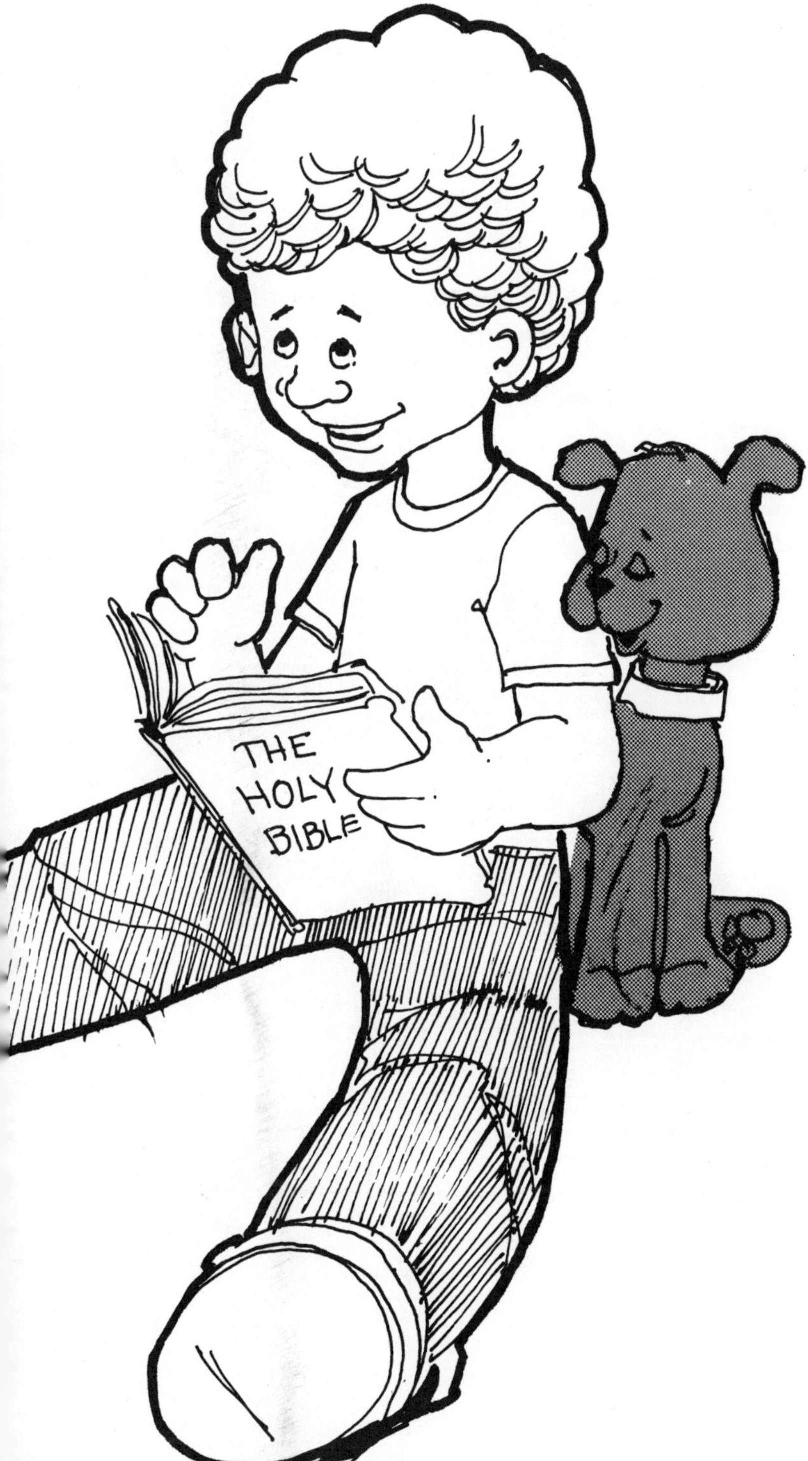
THE HOLY BIBLE

## Why were Jesus and his disciples cruel to the corn?

*They pulled its ears.*

## What was Methuselah after he was nine hundred and sixty-eight years old?

*Nine hundred and sixty-nine.*

## Which book of the Bible contains another name for a girl?

*(Gal)-atians.*